Pay It Forward

75 Ideas to Build a Better World

Published by Neuron Publishing
www.neuronpublishing.com
www.LoveBookOnline.com

A little love goes a long way...

Every day we are faced with decisions that can make a difference in someone's life, and we have the power to do something to make that person's day better.

Listed in this book are 75 simple ideas to help improve your life and the lives of others. Everyone shows and responds to love in different ways, so the book is categorized into sections based on the five languages of love: Acts of Service, Quality Time, Giving, Physical Support and Communication.

Choose to make a positive difference by spreading some love today!

· ·

Acts of Service

Volunteering - our time, money
or talents - can have a very
positive effect on the lives of
others as well as increase our
own life satisfaction. You can
help out an organization, a
neighbor, a friend, or a stranger.
Just help someone.

Sign up and train for an event that benefits a cause.

You'll feel great about helping others, while improving your own health in the process.

What event did I train for?

....

....

When did I do it?

....

....

Whom did it benefit?

....

....

7

Clean up litter at your local park.

Living in a clean environment helps our earth, wildlife, and ourselves. Others who see you may be inspired to clean up as well.

Where did I clean up?

Whom did it benefit?

How could I inspire others to help next time?

8

Watch someone's house while they are away.

Take care of their pet, pick up their mail, take out their garbage, etc. Helping others will give you confidence and give them peace of mind.

Whose house did I watch?

Why did I decide to help them?

How can I help them even more?

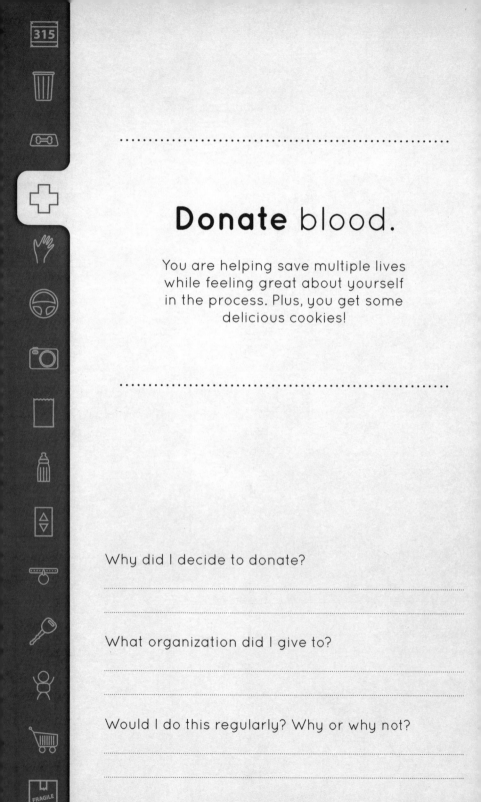

Donate blood.

You are helping save multiple lives while feeling great about yourself in the process. Plus, you get some delicious cookies!

Why did I decide to donate?

What organization did I give to?

Would I do this regularly? Why or why not?

Help someone in need.

Seek out ways to brighten the day of people in your life. You could feed the homeless, cheer up someone who is down on their luck, or give a close friend a shoulder to cry on.

Whom have I helped?

....

....

Why did I decide to help?

....

....

Whom could I help in the future?

....

....

Drive someone to the airport.

Also pick them up, if you can. You can take the burden off of a stressed traveler and make their day just a bit easier.

Whom did I drive?

When did I do this? How did I feel?

How else could I reduce someone's stress?

Offer to **take a photo** for someone.

Notice a family on vacation, or a couple out to dinner? The photo you take will give them a nice memory of the event.

Whom did I take a picture for?

....

....

Where did I take it?

....

....

How did they react? How did that make me feel?

....

....

Help your cashier
bag your groceries.

You're saving time for the
cashier, the people in line, and
yourself all while helping to
make the cashier's job easier.

When did I do this?

How did the cashier react?

Is there any other way I could help service-people?

Offer to **babysit** for someone.

Watching someone's kids
helps them find time to
run errands, relax, or just
reconnect with each other.

Whom did I babysit for?

....
....

How did it benefit them?

....
....

How often could I do this? Whom else could I help?

....
....

Hold open a door or elevator for someone.

This simple gesture could save someone time or the struggle of opening a door with an armful of things.

Where did I do this?

How did they react?

What else could I do to improve someone's day?

Adopt a rescue pet.

Giving an abandoned animal a second chance has many benefits; including the positive boost you'll feel from rescuing it and getting a new companion in the process.

What shelter did I adopt from?

....

....

How did I choose my pet?

....

....

How did I feel after adopting?

....

....

Run an errand
for someone.

This is a simple way to show someone you care about them. Picking up groceries, washing a car, or dropping off mail are all things you can do to help someone out.

Whom did I help?

Is there anyone else I could do tasks for?

How else could I help others in this way?

18

Sponsor a child, a wild animal, or both.

Helping to provide the basic necessities to a child or animal is a great gesture of love and comfort.

How did I accomplish this task?

....

....

Whom/what did I sponsor?

....

....

Would I do this again? Why?

....

....

Let someone check out in front of you at the store.

Doing this shows that you're willing to sacrifice your time for someone else, and makes their day easier.

When did I do this?

Why did I do it at that particular moment?

How else could I give up my time to help others?

Help a friend move without thinking twice.

Helping a friend or family member with a task as huge as this shows them just how much you care, and makes them feel special.

Whom did I help?

....

....

Is there anyone else I could do tasks for?

....

....

How did I feel after helping?

....

....

FRAGILE

Quality Time

Sharing our time with someone else shows them that we love them and also shows that we are willing to make them a priority in our life. When we spend quality time with others, we create a deeper bond and learn to be more comfortable around them.

Don't ask if someone needs help, **just jump in and help them.**

Most times when we ask, people will say "no thank you". So just jump in to help! Grab a spoon and start stirring the sauce at a dinner party or help a neighbor carry their groceries.

How did I help without being asked?

....

....

How did the person I helped feel?

....

....

How would I feel if someone did this for me?

....

....

....

Spend time with a grandparent.

Our grandparents always have the best stories! Sit down with an elderly loved one and ask to learn recipes, hear about family history, or gain from their wisdom.

....

Whom did I spend time with? How?

What did we learn from each other?

Whom else could I spend time with?

Make **quality time** for your pet.

Animals need love and attention just like we do, so make time for your pet. Spending quality time with a furry friend calms your nerves and gives you a sense of comfort.

What routines did I adopt to do this?

walk the dogs, lay with them on the couch, talk to them

How do I feel when I spend time with my pet?

relaxed and loved

Could I meet someone to do things with our pets?

meet someone at the park, walk the dogs with Jordan

Coach or mentor kids.

Children need someone to look up to, so why not you? Share your talents with a younger generation, even if you don't have a child that is involved.

What organization did I get involved in?

Which talents was I able to offer them?

How do I feel when I help children grow?

Create traditions.

Bonding is more than just
time spent together; it creates
confidence in children and comfort
in adults. Make a family game
night, pizza day in the office, or
monthly movie night with friends.

What tradition(s) did I create? With whom?

How did I feel creating this bond with others?

What additional traditions could I create?

Have a meaningful conversation with someone over coffee.

Visit with someone who you know would enjoy the company and creating some lasting bonds.

Whom did I meet? Where?

What did we talk about?

Would I make this a regular visit?

Put away your cell phone during time with others.

Showing people that their time is precious to you makes them feel special and builds a strong bond.

How did I feel after putting my phone away?

How often do I normally check it when I'm out?

What other devices could I temporarily give up?

Randomly **surprise your kids** with a trip to the zoo.

Do it on a school day! Extend this gesture to any children in your life. They'll be excited and feel special to have a day just for them.

Whom did I surprise?

How did they react?

How else could I surprise them?

Take your mom or dad to an event.

Make time to take a loved one to an event that they would enjoy. The event is the reason for going, but the time spent together is the true gift.

What event did I take them to?

How do I feel when I spend time with them?

What else could we do together?

Next time you have a party, **invite your neighbors.**

You may build a new relationship: someone to help in emergencies, a walking buddy, or a new friend to confide in.

Whom did I get to know better?

How did I do it?

How can I continue building a friendship with them?

Enjoy a talk with someone you rarely see.

Sit down with them and ask open-ended questions. Grow the conversation, as well as the relationship.

Whom did I have a conversation with?

What did we talk about?

How did I feel afterward?

Make time
for friends.

Friends help you succeed,
grow your confidence, and
support you. Schedule time
each week or month to have
a nice evening with friends.

How did I make time to see them?

How often did I normally spend time with them?

How could we become even closer?

Start a conversation with someone.

When the opportunity arises, strike up a conversation with someone you don't know. You may find you have something in common!

Whom did I do this with?

What did we talk about?

How did I feel afterward?

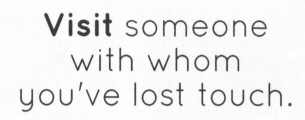

Visit someone with whom you've lost touch.

Whether life just gets in the way or you've had a falling-out, take the time to get in touch with someone whom you haven't talked to in a while.

Whom did I visit?

How did they react?

How did I feel after visiting them?

Spend time
with a neighbor over cookies.

Our neighbors help with our kids, our homes, and our pets. Bake cookies or make a fruit plate and head over for some one-on-one time.

How did I spend time with a neighbor?

How often do I normally communicate with them?

How else could I build my relationship with them?

Giving

We all know how it feels to receive a gift: we feel loved, appreciated, and sometimes surprised! Giving a gift can evoke those same emotions, plus we feel great about ourselves for making someone else so happy.

Leave a dollar in a random place.

The feeling of finding
unexpected money will bring
joy to whomever finds it.

When did I do this? Where?

How did I feel afterward?

How do I think the person finding it reacted?

Offer change to someone at a store.

We all know the feeling of
being a few cents short. Helping
someone who is in a pinch can
relax them, and make the rest
of their day run smoothly.

Where did I do this?

How did that person react?

Would I do it again?

Make someone a playlist of **inspiring** music.

Besides the mood-enhancing effects of music, a homemade playlist from a friend makes a sentimental and thoughtful gift.

Whom did I do this for?

What songs did I include? Why?

Could I make more for other people?

Research a charity and **make a donation.**

Do some digging to find an organization that you believe in, and donate - money, clothing, time...whatever you can spare!

What charity did I choose?

How did I contribute?

Is there another way I could help out?

Give stamps to people waiting at the post office.

Being at the post office is a stressful time, so why not help out? You'll save people time and money, plus unexpected acts of kindness are the best ones.

How did they react?

What other items could I give away?

Would I do this again?

Frame a good picture you took of someone and give it to them.

They'll appreciate the thought behind it and have something memorable to decorate with.

Whom did I take a picture of?

....

....

Where was the picture taken?

....

....

How could I make it even more personalized?

....

....

Buy a round of drinks for a random table.

Tell your server that you'd like to pick up the round. They'll greatly appreciate the gesture, and most likely pay it forward on their own time.

Where did I do this?

How did I feel afterward?

How often could I do this?

Donate clothes that you no longer wear.

Try not to limit it just to clothing! We all have things we don't need anymore, but to someone else it could be a necessity.

What charity did I donate to?

savers and/or local families

How often could I donate?

pretty often, everytime I come home

What else could I donate?

toys, books

Give books to a local school or library.

Most schools have limited funds, so donations help out in a big way. Teachers will appreciate having new stories, and kids will learn more by having a larger variety of options.

What schools/libraries did I give to?

What books (or supplies) did I donate?

How else could I get involved in my community?

Offer unused coupons to the people in line.

Getting an unexpected discount is an awesome feeling! You could also leave a coupon on the shelf near the product itself.

When/where did I do this?

Could I do it more often?

Would I cut coupons just for this purpose?

Take cold water to sanitation workers on a hot day.

This also goes for anyone who works long hours outdoors. Laborious work is taxing, and receiving unexpected refreshment could make someone's day and prevent dehydration.

Whom did I do this for? How did they react?

....

....

How did I feel afterwards?

....

....

Whom else could I do this for?

....

....

Create a gift
for someone.

Instead of buying the next gift
you give, make an item that
means something to you and
the receiver. It's a sentiment
that will be cherished forever.

How did I put my talents to use?

Whom did I make something for?

Could I create for other causes (i.e. charities)?

Once in a while, **double the amount** you tip someone.

Being in the service industry is one of the toughest jobs out there. Giving double what they'd normally expect for a tip shows that they (and their work) are appreciated.

When did I do this?

Whom do I normally tip (i.e. hairdresser, barista)?

How often could I do this?

Ask for donations
to a charity for your birthday.

There are many people out there who need help, so why not sacrifice a little for them? Try to do this for any event in which you receive gifts.

What holiday did I do this for?

What organization did I help?

How else could I get involved?

Share
with others.

Share your time, money, or possessions. Studies have shown that the act of giving to someone increases happiness and contentment in ourselves, and makes us feel rewarded in the process.

How did I share with others (i.e. talents, money)?

What other opportunities arise for me to do this?

How could I inspire others to share as well?

Physical Support

Gently touching someone's
arm, easing the burden of
physical pain, or showing your
love intimately are all ways
of expressing love physically.
Showing affection by contact
increases our relationships
with others and makes both the
person you are touching and
ourselves feel loved.

Give someone a hug.

Studies show that a simple hug is a universal sign of compassion; by opening your arms and exposing vulnerable parts of your body, you are displaying a symbol of trust.

Whom did I hug today?

....

....

How do I feel when I receive/give a hug?

....

....

How else could I show compassion to others?

....

....

Hold your partner's hand during a walk.

A little PDA never hurt anyone. Showing your partner love by simply holding hands creates a deeper intimate bond between you two.

What kind of affection did I show?

How often do I show my partner affection?

How else could I increase our intimacy?

Give up your seat for someone else.

Even if they aren't elderly or pregnant. Letting someone have your seat shows respect and makes them feel cared for. Keep an eye out for anyone who may need a seat.

Where did I do this?

Could I pay more attention to other's needs?

What else could I do for strangers?

Give your partner an **unexpected kiss.**

Technically, kissing floods the brain with dopamine, an internal chemical that is released when you're doing something highly pleasurable. Plus, it increases intimacy between you two.

How did he/she react?

Did this bring us closer together?

How else could I show unexpected attention?

Snuggle with your pet.

It's been proven that playing or relaxing with a pet has huge health benefits, including decreasing stress, increasing happiness and even lowering the risk of heart attacks.

How did I do this?

How often could I do this?

How do I feel afterwards?

Give someone a **butterfly kiss.**

With thousands of nerve endings in the face, the feeling of eyelashes "fluttering" on the skin will make anyone feel wonderful.

Whom did I give a butterfly kiss to?

Did I get a kiss back?

How did it feel?

Offer someone a
shoulder to cry on.

Showing concern for others makes
them feel comforted and understood.
Next time someone you know is
having a rough day, offer to listen
and empathize with their situation.

Whom did I offer support to?

How did it make them feel?

What else could I do to help others?

Shake hands with people you meet.

Historically, the handshake originated as a gesture of peace by demonstrating that the hand holds no weapon. Nowadays, it's a sign of respect and welcoming.

When did I last do this?

Do I feel closer to someone afterwards?

What other kinds of touch show respect?

Start a friendly
pillow fight.

This is a fun way to release primal energy. In some cities, *International Pillow Fight Day* is celebrated with thousands of people engaging in a massive pillow fight.

When did I start a surprise pillow fight?

Who was involved?

How did it end?

Push a child on a swing.

Spending time with a child can increase their confidence and success rate, and helps you remember how to be a kid again.

Whom did I take to a park (or spend time with)?

How else could I spend my time with youth?

How else can I embrace my inner child?

Help someone **carry something** heavy for them.

Everyone appreciates a helping hand. If they are struggling to carry something, take it off their hands. You could also help reduce emotional weight, such as a heavy burden.

Whom did I help?

When did I do this?

How did the person I helped react?

Shovel sidewalks
for someone.

Shoveling is a great cardio workout, but can be dangerous to people with heart conditions or the elderly. If you're healthy and capable, help your neighbors by clearing their sidewalks too.

Whom did I do this for?

How often could I help them?

What else could I do (i.e. mow their lawn)?

Give your partner an **unexpected** shoulder massage.

Increase intimacy with this act. Ask how much pressure they like before you start, and use a lotion or oil to help reduce friction, making the experience more enjoyable.

How did my partner react?

Did this bring me closer to my partner?

How else could I surprise him/her with touch?

Give someone
a boost.

Lift a child to shoot a basket or
help someone deepen a stretch
after a workout. The most
appreciated acts can also be
the most simple ones.

Whom did I do this for?

....
....

How often during daily life could I do this?

....
....

How did they react?

....
....

Give someone a **pat on the back.**

Everyone loves appreciation and praise for a job well done. Try giving compliments publicly as well, to show credit where credit is due.

Whom did I give credit to?

....

....

How often could I do this?

....

....

How else could I show appreciation?

....

....

Communication

Whether it's a simple hello
to a stranger or a deep
conversation with an old friend,
communicating with others
helps build relationships. Try
some of these ideas with people
you meet or know, and see how
the friendships evolve!

Forgive
someone who has wronged you.

Forgiveness has many benefits for you
and those around you. It can lower
blood pressure, increase positivity and
reduce stress. So, just let it go!

Whom did I forgive?

....
....

How did it feel to me and the other person?

....
....

How else could I let go of negative emotions?

....
....

When out for a run or walk, **say hello** to people you pass.

Acts of courteousness create a sense of camaraderie during a time when most people focus only on their task at hand. It also shows you are friendly and approachable.

How did this simple gesture make me feel?

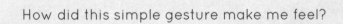

Does this bring me closer to others?

Can I go a step further and run with someone?

Randomly contact someone to **tell them why you care.**

Call, text, email, or send a letter telling someone exactly why you love them. They'll feel loved and respected because of this random gesture.

Whom did I contact?

Why do I love them?

Whom else could I contact?

···

Comment to someone if they have well-behaved children.

Parenting is challenging. A sincere compliment from a stranger can make a parent feel proud and increase their confidence that they are doing a great job.

···

Where did I do this?

....
....

How did they react?

....
....

How else could I make parents feel appreciated?

....
....

Compliment
someone.

Giving someone a compliment is an easy way to lift the spirits of others, and lift your own in the process. Extend this to strangers, coworkers, family, and friends.

Whom did I compliment? For what?

....
....

How did it make them feel?

....
....

How else could I brighten someone's day?

....
....

Send a thank you card to someone who inspired you.

Think about someone in your life who has taught you something or helped you through a tough time. Take a moment to send them a note extending your gratitude.

How did I thank somebody?

Whom else has inspired me throughout life?

Whom else could I send a letter to?

Do something nice
for yourself.

When you feel happy, you are in a
better state of mind to make others
happy. And that happiness can be
spread, from city to state to country.

What did I do for myself?

Could I make it a regular event?

How does it positively affect others?

Truly listen to people when they talk.

Being attentive lets someone know that you really care about what they have to say and builds a stronger bond. And someday, they will return the favor.

How did I show better listening skills?

In what other ways could I be attentive to people?

How do I feel when I focus more on others?

Make silly faces
at a child standing in a line.

Be a little goofy sometimes!
Life can get dull if you
don't take the time to
embrace your inner child.

How did the child react?

....

....

How else could I bring out my inner child?

....

....

Are there others in my life I can be goofy with?

....

....

Send a letter to someone in the armed services.

They do so much for us without expecting our gratitude. Sending a letter explaining why you appreciate them can make all the effort they're putting forth worth it.

What did I say to thank him/her?

Do I know someone in the military?

How else could I thank him/her (i.e. care package)?

Leave your server a **nice note** along with their tip.

Being a server can be a tough job, and a simple act of appreciation can make their day. You could also tell their manager how well of a job they did.

When/where did I do this?

How do I think the server might react?

How else could I show appreciation to my server?

Leave a nice note on a stranger's car.

Imagine having a bad day, then seeing a random note that simply reads "Smile". How would you feel? Try doing this for someone; chances are it will make them feel better.

Where did I leave a note? What did it say?

How often could I do this?

Could I involve friends to make this a big project?

Think before you speak.

Not only what you say, but how you say it, can have a huge impact on someone's day. Choose your words carefully and make your point clear and concise.

What situation did I do this?

....

....

How can I express myself in a better way?

....

....

Could I try to speak less and listen more? How?

....

....

Smile at people.

Better yet, make them laugh!
It's been shown that people
who laugh and smile often
have less stress and better
relationships with others.

How did I feel when smiling at others?

Do people smile back?

How can I make someone laugh?

Teach your children to spread the love.

Lead by example. Show younger generations that their actions can have a positive effect on the world, and in turn, on the next generations to come.

How can I teach this to a child in my life?

....

....

What organizations could I get them involved in?

....

....

If I don't have kids, who can I positively influence?

....

....

About LoveBook™:

We are a group of individuals
who want to spread love in all
its forms. We believe love fuels
the world and every relationship
is important. We hope this book
helps build on that belief.

CPSIA information can be obtained at www.ICGtesting.com
Printed in the USA
BVIW12n2054020116
431495BV00014B/263